Òran Uisge
Wildflower Meadow

Nature Poems

By
Sue Wood

Grosvenor House
Publishing Limited

This book is published by
Grosvenor House Publishing Ltd
Link House
140 The Broadway, Tolworth, Surrey, KT6 7HT.
www.grosvenorhousepublishing.co.uk

A CIP record for this book
is available from the British Library

ISBN 978-1-83975-537-8

Dedication

To my beautiful grandchildren
From
Granny Skye.

Acknowledgements

I would like to thank the following friends and
family for their help and support
Dale Kendrick for his editing skills
Warren Wood, Jill Simpson and Kim Louise Wood
for their continual support
Warren Wood, Jill Simpson and Kersty Lockhart
for their photographs.

Robyn and Erika for their love of nature.

Contents

Nature Poems

Walk in the Woods

Down the long lane, beneath the blue sky,
I step into the wood with the canopy high
The track is adorned with flowery dells,
With wonderful scents from sapphire bells.
Through dappled shade the ferns grow bright,
Cheering the gloom with emerald light.
I hear the birds sing on branches high,
As their shapes silhouette against the sky.
The winding track weaves through the trees,
As their leaves quiver and move in the breeze.
Mossy logs lie and cover the ground,
While wood anemones speckle the mound.
A balmy fragrance fills the air,
An exquisite perfume could not compare.
The woods are delightful, at this time of year,
With Springtime sounds and scents in the air.

Buttercup by Robyn aged 5 years

Buttercup Days

Buttercup blooms with sunlight glow,
Delicate yellow they display and show.
Standing tall above feather grass,
Waving their hues to all who pass.
Holding a bloom under a chin,
You do love butter! a childish grin.
A golden reflection so small and light,
Glows on the chin, which shines so bright.
Buttercups take me back to the days,
I was free and careless in so many ways.
(For Robyn)

Call from the Wild

Across the moor where the land is wild,
Bog cotton and reeds on every side.
Wind swept and fresh, with freedom to roam,
Solitude and peace away from home.
Rest in stillness, a solitary time,
The world is calm, a moment so fine.
The silence is broken, with a haunting cry,
A curious call with a pitch, so high.
An eerie song from a distant rise,
Curlew calling, the song of the wild.
Mysterious and haunting, music to love,
A beguiling silhouette, glides above.
He searches the moor for a suitable site,
To build a nest in a place just right.
Again, he calls to his mate close by,
A courtship ritual as they soar and fly.
Early Spring, this time of year,
Curlews delight with their song they share.

Morning Dew

This is a moment to stop and stare,
In total solitude with no one to share.
Sunshine beams with rays so clear,
Breath-clouds rise in a cool dawn air.
Delicate mist swirls and floats,
Glistening the flowers watery coats.
Strings of gossamer crisscross the lea,
Like jewelled necklaces for all to see.
Warmth rises up and lifts the dew,
While tiny beetles sip the brew.
Marmalade hoverfly waits for heat,
And basks on a reed, a perfect seat.
As the dew wanes, the air is warm,
The insects rise, dance and perform.
Absorbed in the meadow at its best,
While taking a moment to gaze at rest.

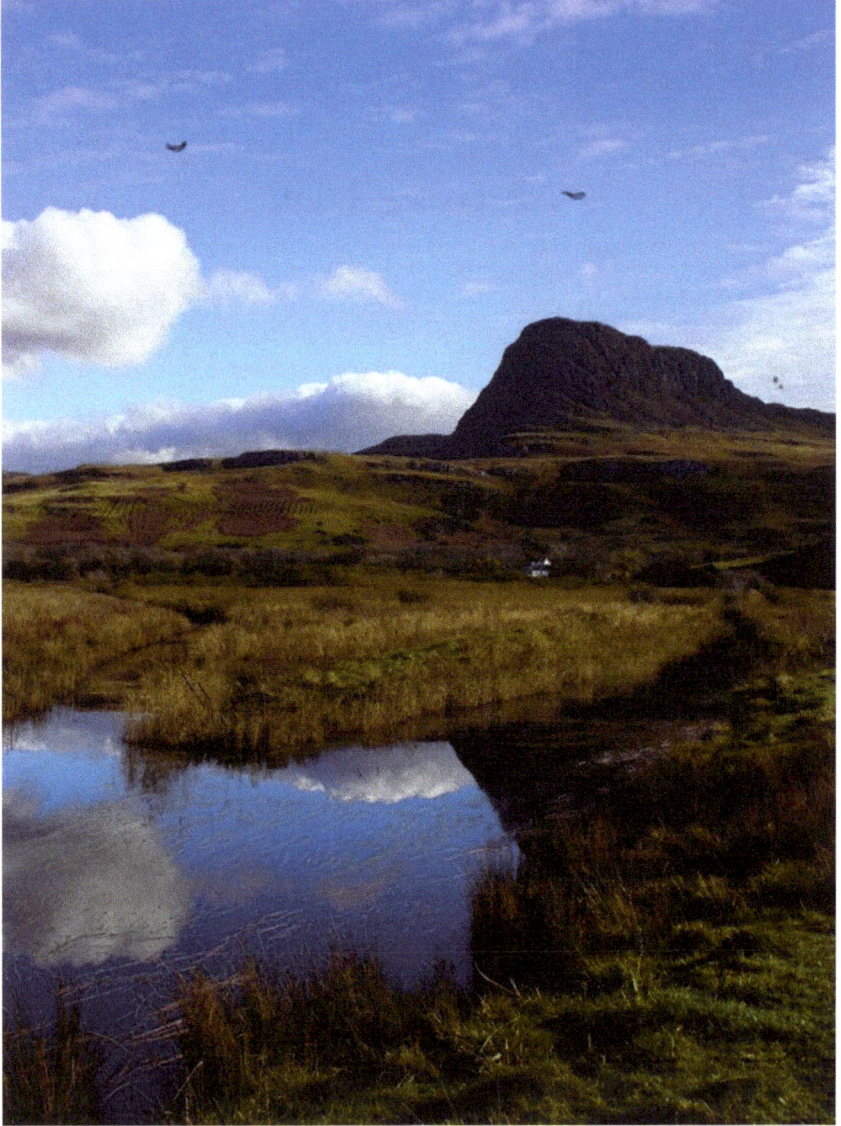

Skylark Choir

Spring has arrived with warming air,
The rain has ceased and the sky is clear.
A gentle breeze is swirling around,
As tiny daisies poke through the ground.
Relaxing now…then a pleasing surprise!
The lark has returned over the rise.
This tiny brown bird, so hard to see,
Yet filling the air with a song so free.
He flies up high and sings his tune
He glides to the moor but, all too soon.
His rivals take off and are rising high
A splendid chorus as the minutes pass by.
Oh…this peace and tranquility is mine
This skylark choir, musically divine.

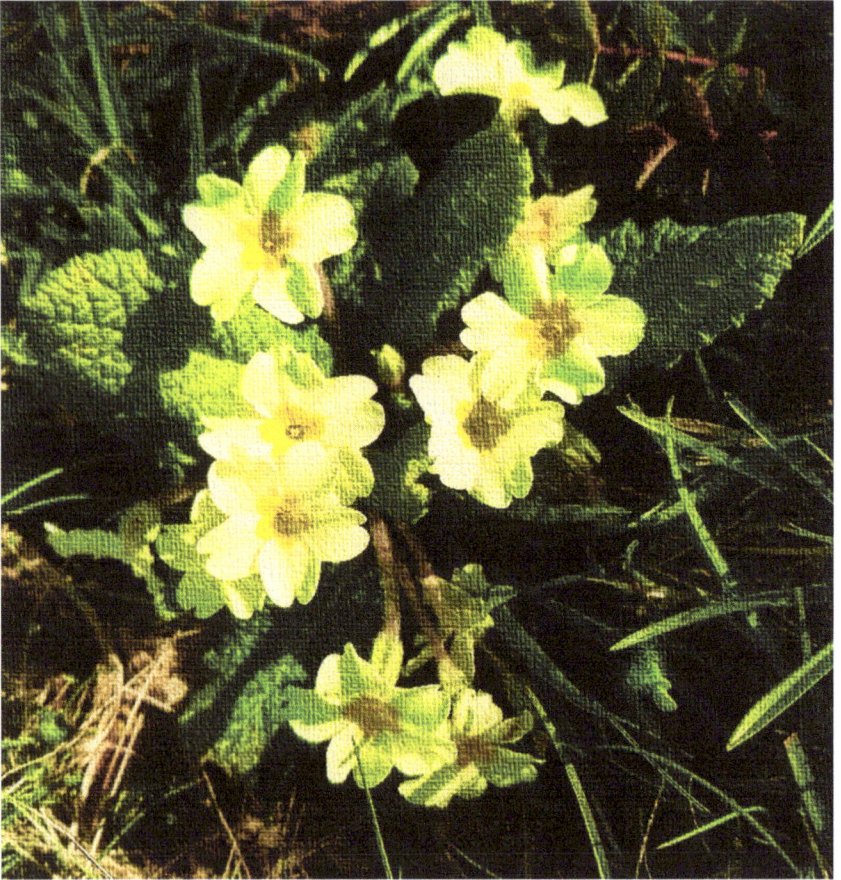

Primroses in Spring

Early Spring....... and I yearn and ponder,
I stroll up the lane, in aimless wander.
The hedgerow is dull from winter's rest,
I long for blooms of lemony zest.
I see a glow, beneath the tall tree,
A cluster of blooms, so vibrant to see.
Sunshine beams amongst the shade,
Lights up the void within the glade.
Cheerful blooms yellow and bright,
Sunny bowls of golden delight.
So, stirring and inspiring to view,
Primroses glittered with morning dew.

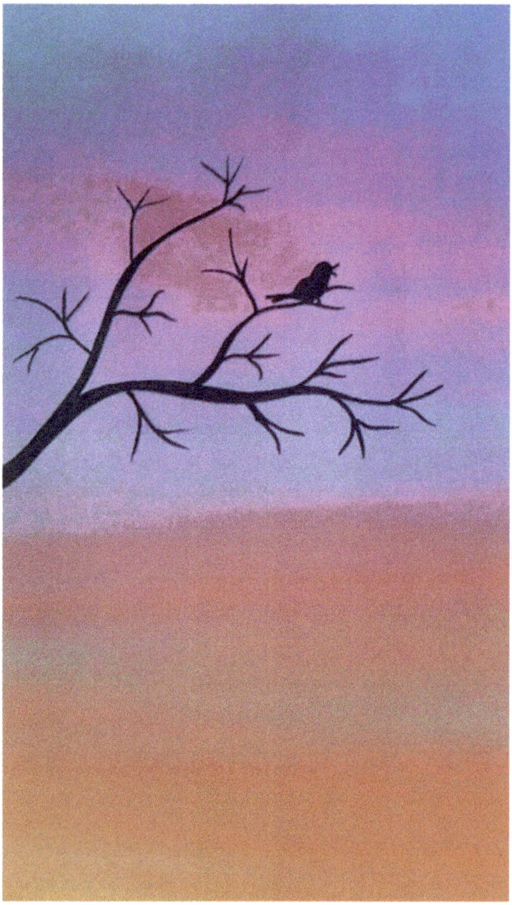

The Chorus at Dawn

May is a month to cherish each year,
With the dawn chorus, birds love to share.
From breaking light, they start their trill,
With this blissful choir, our hearts will thrill.
The Blackbird and Robin start their call,
With many followers big and small.
They fill the meadow with tunes, so sweet
An orchestral performance could not compete.
They sing out loud to claim their ground,
A warning to others from all around.
Attracting a mate to build a nest,
And rearing their broods, while feeding with zest,
They fill our world with their melodic tune,
Lifting our spirits, but all too soon,
Their chicks will fledge, to find new ground.
And the songs will change to a quiet sound.
The year will pass then, time for the Spring,
When the birds wake up and start to sing.

Chimney Sweeper Moth

Jet-black wings drift with grace,
Sooty -flashes embellish this place.
Diamond tips, bright and on view,
Glint in the meadow; a vibrant hue.
Frothy pignut with creamy foam,
Your feeding larder and favoured home.
You flutter and fly near to the ground,
On the wildflower lea, where you are found.

Harebell

Delicate bonnet of baby-blue,
Iridescent glow from misty hues.
Your head droops down to hide your face,
As you quiver and tremble with gentle grace.
Summer breezes allow you to dance,
Holding my gaze in a spellbound trance.

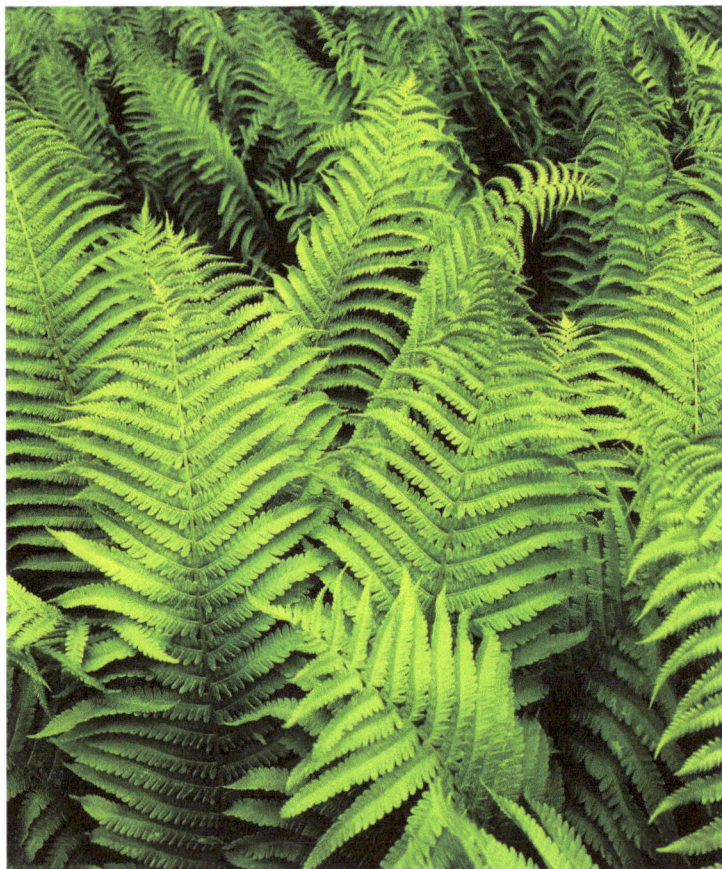

Dancing Ferns

Uncoiling their fronds and growing up high,
They tremble and quiver and reach for the sky.
Leaves like lace adorning the gloom,
Sweep through the wood like a magical broom.
Acid green plumes, a vibrant sight,
Fill the woods with emerald light.
Silver grey backs hiding from view,
Speckled with spores of caramel hues.
A swaying dance the audience can see,
A spectacular show, natural and free.

Dandelion Time

Dandelion seed heads, like gossamer orbs,
Sway in the breeze back and forth.
Three or more, ornate the trail,
With glossy leaves green and pale.
Children pick their stems for fun,
While playing outside in the midday sun.
Puff and blow with all their might,
One o' clock, two o' clock, time just right.
As years pass by and memories fade,
Nostalgic thoughts of the games we played.
Dandelion reminiscing, happy and sweet,
Great moments to cherish, a childhood treat.

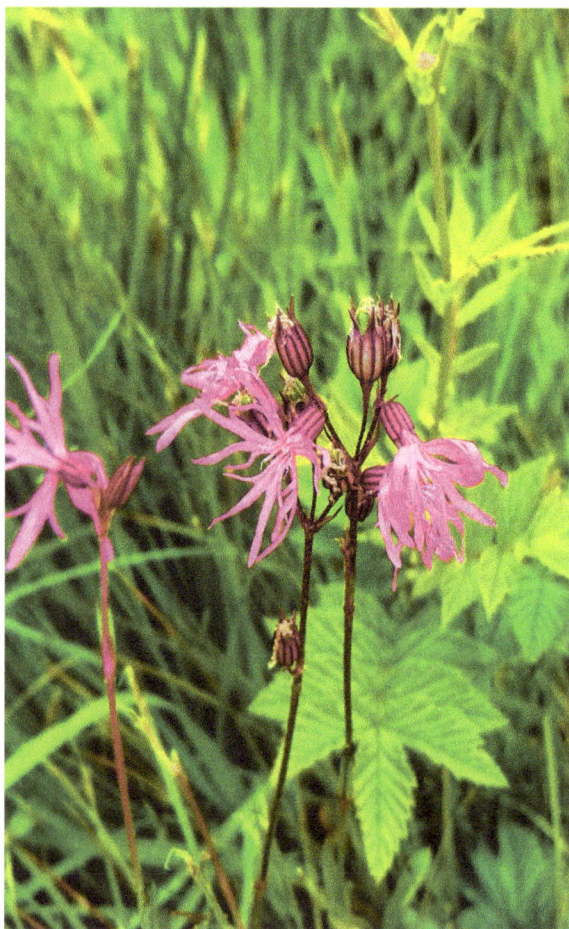

Flowers of Summer

Lady's mantle sparkling with dew,
Speedwell shining an iridescent blue.
Shepherds purse speckled with white,
Lilac and gold, the tiny eyebright.
Gallant soldier and meadowsweet,
Honeysuckle balmy and sweet.
Golden ragwort the crofters' foe,
Ragged robin with bright pink glow.
Cuckoo flower and tall foxgloves,
Majestic orchid and fox and cubs.
Slender thistle with purple blooms,
Yellow hues from hawkweed and brooms.
Regal kingcups and heath bedstraw,
Beautiful flowers with many more.
Colourful names with hues so bright
Light up our world with dazzling delight.
Exquisite fragrance fills the air,
An artist's palette for all to share.

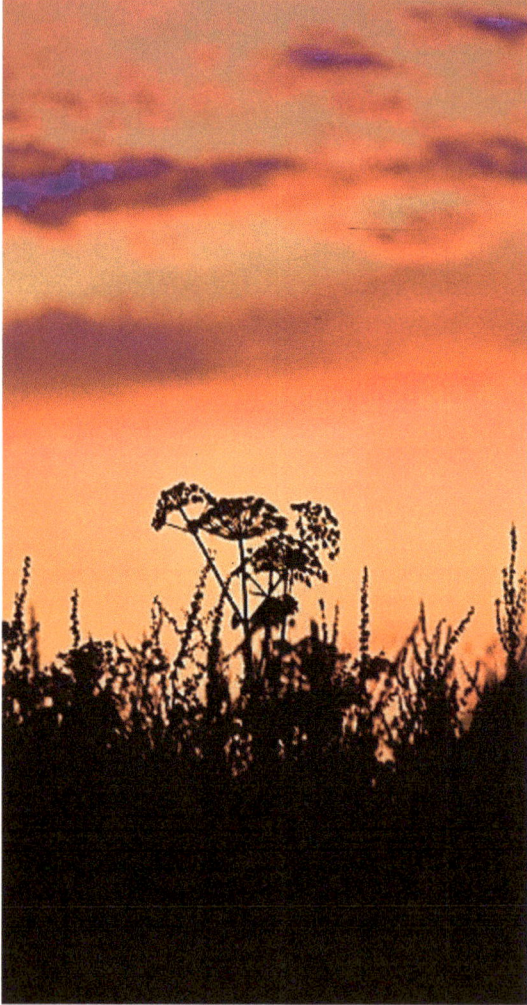

Midsummer Night

To settle and rest then, close your eyes,
Absorbing the sweet air with gentle sighs.
The dew is falling with moist delight,
To cool the meadow, in the fading light.
Scents of meadowsweet and orchid ascend,
Through the night air like, a heady friend.
To smell the honeysuckle balmy and sweet,
And crush wood sage beneath your feet.
Hear the snipe drum and glide to the ground,
With his enigmatic and haunting sound.
A gentle bee forages with a hum,
Before the light is finally done.
The magic evening is closing down,
With fading light and evocative sounds.
Oh! To linger silently, forever,
Cradled in this Midsummer treasure.

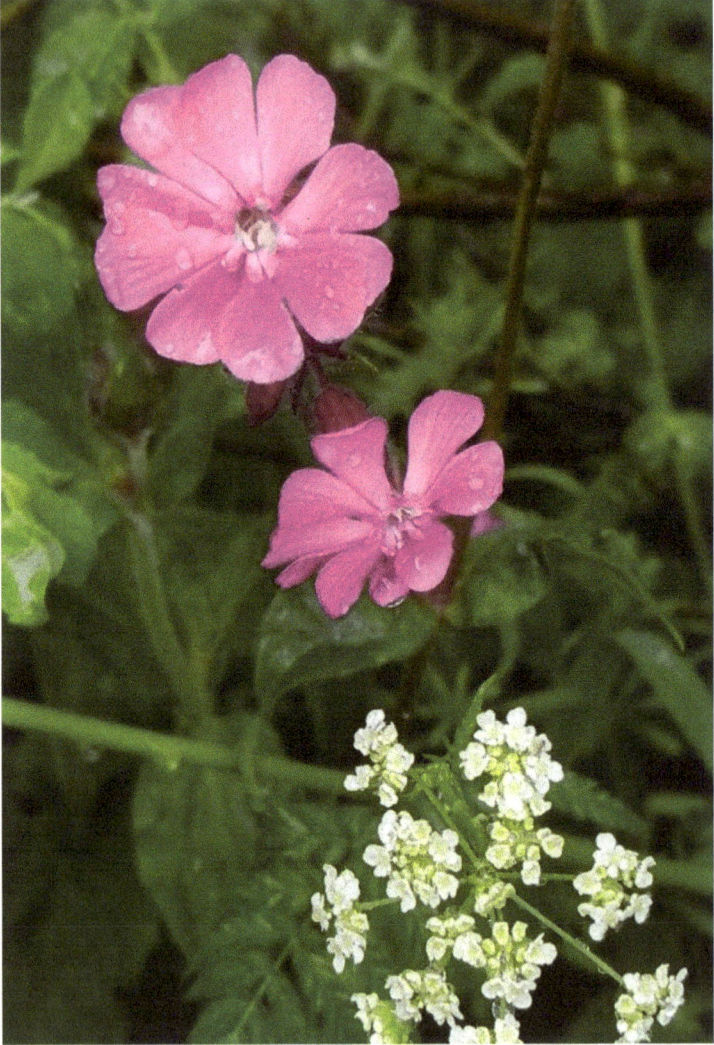

Summer Rain

Hot balmy day, airless and close,
Dark ominous clouds, above they rose.
Casting dark shadows all around,
The air is still, without a sound.
A cooling shower trickles and runs,
Then pits and pats like, tiny drums.
Summer rain brings relief to all,
From heat and dust, as droplets fall.
A vibrant rainbow adorns the sky,
An arching spectrum, way up high.
Steamy air ascends and climbs,
Creative mist in swirling lines.
Leaves and petals, luminous and bright,
Glowing so fresh, an alluring sight.
A rich sweet fragrance fills the air,
A priceless perfume could not compare.

Along the Lane

The ground warms up in early Spring
When the birds seek mates and start to sing.
Acid green leaves erupt into view,
With fresh Spring colours in multiple hues
Summer arrives with hot balmy air
As butterflies and bees fly without care.
Bursting blooms with scents so sweet,
Enrich this world with a fragrant treat.
The year will pass as the seasons change
With colours and scents in a breath-taking range.

Swallow Season

One day they arrive in a frenzied flight,
On a beautiful morning, with sky so bright.
Swooping and soaring, they show off their skills,
Diving and spinning, they perform at will.
Beaks full of mud from the ground they collect,
Their nest in the eaves, they strive to perfect.
Tirelessly working from dawn until dusk,
They bind their nests; in these they must trust.
Laying their eggs and raising their brood,
Their toil continues, as they search for food.
Hunting in flight, with acrobatic flair,
Butterflies and moths come out (if they dare).
The season is short, and soon they are gone,
To a much warmer climate, where they belong.

Wildflower Meadow

Òran Uisge you haven of peace.
Surrounding my form with a silken fleece.
Your flowers burst from an emerald sea,
Amazing my eyes with the beauty I see.
A spectrum of colour in the early dawn light,
Brings warmth to my mood from floral delight.
I wish you could last for the whole of the year,
But alas, you cannot, and the loss I must bear.
Farewell until spring, when you reappear,
In a carpet of hues, your gift brings me cheer.

Willow Confetti

The warm breeze travels across the lea,
Circling, turning, wild and free.
It carries the mayflies up in the air,
Searching for mates to dance and share.
Amongst their courtship, floating high,
The willow confetti obscures the sky.
Summer snow speckles, downy and light,
Reflect the sunbeams, in vibrant delight.
Mayflies perform a dancing soiree
Amid willow confetti, wondrous to see.

Where the River Sings

The river serenely sings and flows,
Nearby the meadow where wildflowers grow.
Downy willow seeds float in the air,
Then land on the meadow without a care.
The mayflies dance and sway in the breeze,
While gossamer threads adorn the trees.
A scent of honeysuckle fills the lea,
As bees are foraging wild and free.
The air is warm and the rays are bright,
Flooding the meadow in radiant light.

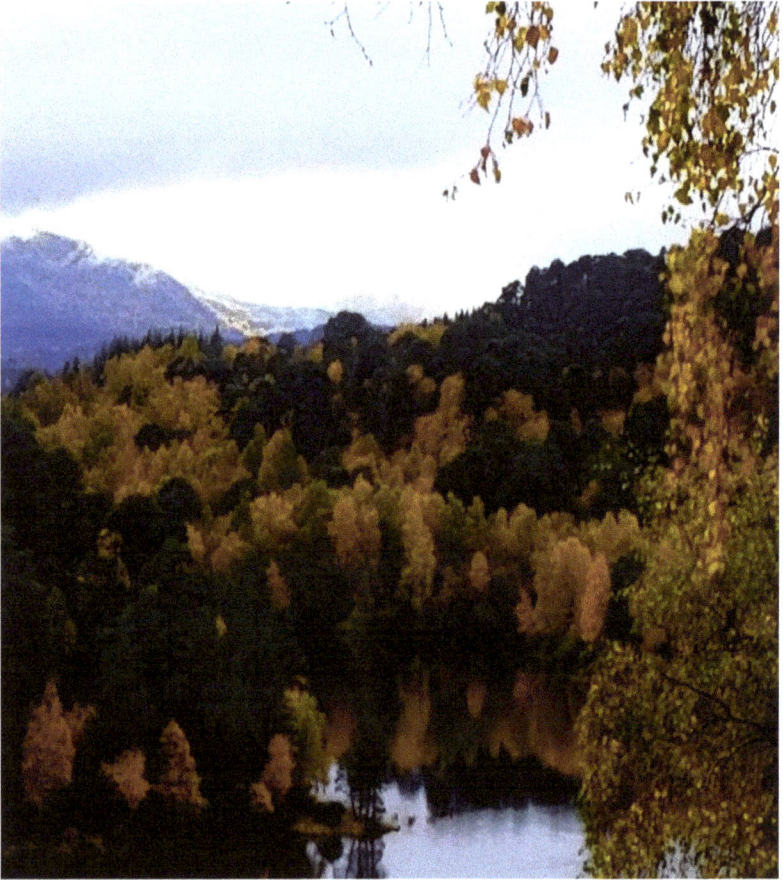

Autumn Glory

Swirling mist covers the land,
Shrouding trees, tall and grand.
Glimpses of sunbeams light the show,
Of Autumn colours, a spectacular glow.
An artist's palette, of vibrant delight,
Which daubs the wood, a glorious sight.
Red and orange, yellow and gold,
An Autumn treat with hues so bold.
Swirling flakes, floating around,
While a crunching carpet covers the ground.
A pleasant aroma fills the air,
A seasonal display, the woodlands share.

Rambling Briars

Rambling and twisting above the
ground, with spiky thorns to protect,
they surround. Numerous creatures forage
through leaves, these tiny fur rodents, the
silent thieves. Relishing juices, your fruits
do share, nourishing their forms in the
Autumn air. Ruby-red jewels shining so
bright, adorning your stems with
scarlet delight. Thrushes and wrens devour your
fruits, protected from thorns in
feathery suits. An Autumn banquet you
do share while, sustaining small creatures
throughout the year.

Dragonfly

You dart about with shimmering wings,
Across the meadow, where the river sings.
Soaring high and dipping low,
Seeking prey, I watch you show,
Your rhythmic flight, precise and fast,
Like an arcane dart, from a time long passed.
My spirits lift, when I hear your hum,
And land on a reed to bask in the sun.
You glisten and gleam, like an emerald gem.
Eyes like jet beads, with piercing lens.
You rise again to greet your mate,
A flash of green at a lightening rate
Courting your mate in a graceful dance,
She harmonises your movements which,
Lengthens my trance.

Memories

Oh…there they are!
A small cluster of jet-black beads.
Hiding in the tangle of arching stems.
Memories of searching with my brother
For those inky berries of delight.
Hunting in a frenzy for the biggest and the juiciest,
Such was our sibling rivalry.
Nettle stings and thorny wounds laced like red stitching
On bear arms and legs.
Then the best part,
Tasting a berry… with divine sweet juice.
A mark of Summer's harvest,
A gift from the Earth.
Days were sunnier, days were longer, with
Happy laughter and childish antics.
But the juicy taste of that first Summer berry,
Is forever etched in my memory.
These nostalgic thoughts of distant
Summers.
With my brother.

Dance of the Barn Owls

The evening draws nigh and the stage is set,
An inspired portrayal awaits us yet.
The jet-black eyes search the ground,
While invisible ears, listen for sound.
Balletic moves and contours to see,
Floating feathers, airless and free.
Cavorting glides and swaying moves,
As night slowly ebbs, the dance improves.
Ghostly white owls float on the breeze,
Performing an encore draped by the trees.
We perceive the ballet for a fleeting time,
An accomplished performance: a vision sublime.

Spinning Her Web

I watch in wonder as you weave and spin,
With gossamer threads, translucent and thin.
A perfect art, through your natural skill,
In this hunting corner your snare will fill.
Silently working in a fascinating show,
With silken strands, pearlescent they glow.
Wave in the breeze, they shimmer and shine,
Your work continues, time after time.
You guard your web, like a fortress manned,
Waiting for prey to clumsily land.
Catching your meal in your quivering snare,
You enjoy your spoils, though your web will tear.
Small silken parcels wrapped up and on show,
Your larder of food lined up in a row.
Your morning begins with your daily chore,
Of weaving and spinning your web, once more.

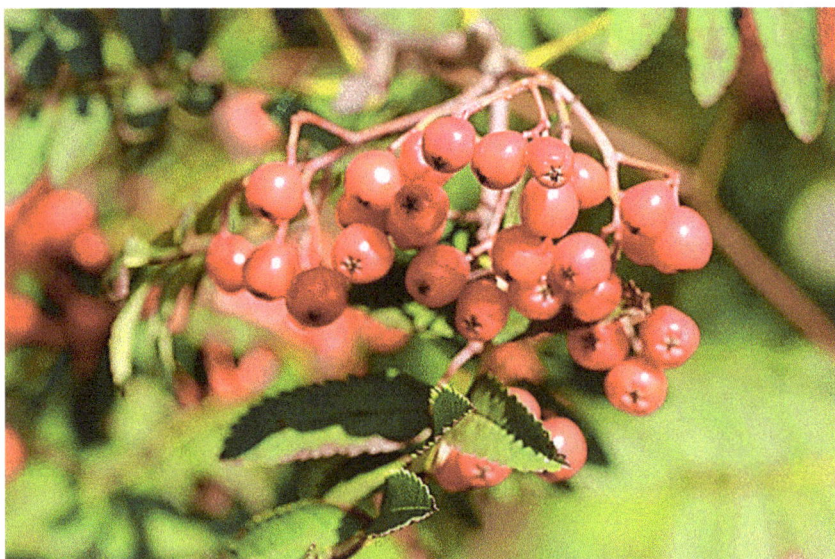

The Rowan Tree

Glorious and graceful, with a striking pose,
From a tiny seed you grew and rose.
Delicate leaves like friendly hands,
Wave to all who watch and stand.
Clusters of flowers, with scents so sweet,
Fill the air with a fragrant treat.
Berries like rubies, red with a shine,
Nourish the birds, throughout Autumn time.
An Autumn special show, you share,
And a stunning time, we await each year.
Celtic myths you bring to our lives,
The tree of life, which makes us wise.
Guarding our families from evil, your goal,
And making us brave to complete your role.
The tree of life so strong and tall,
A seasonal beauty, captivating us all.

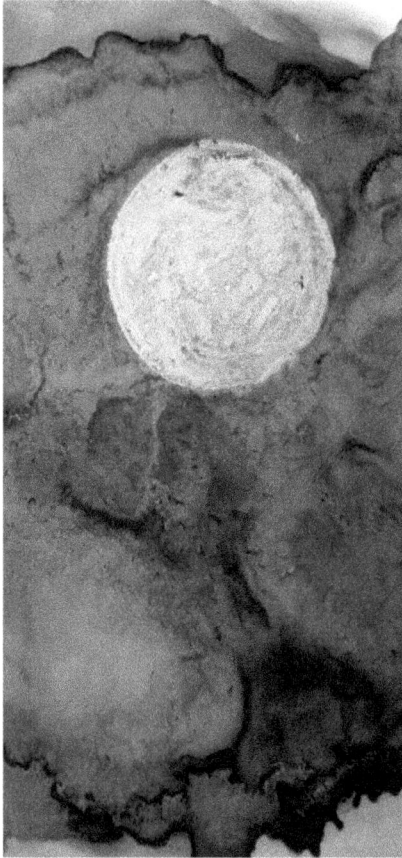

Moonlit Night

On a still, still night, clear and cold,
Skies are dark with stars so bold.
The moon is low, in the ebony air,
A glowing ball, with silver flare.
I watch enthralled, at the shadows you free,
Casting forms for all to see.
I see you rise above the pines,
Like a guiding lamp, which beauty defines.
Moving across the sky with ease,
Clouds pass your orb, upon the breeze.
I think of the time, when the world was new,
Lighting the sky with your silver hue.

Autumn's Fiery Lights

Autumn comes with cooler nights,
Adorning the shrubs with fiery lights.
Gaudy leaves swirling around,
While toadstool rings scatter the ground.

Plumed Spectre

A ghostly sight floats with grace,
As he passes the moons shining face.
This plumed spectre, silent and light,
Searches for prey, throughout the night.
He haunts the land with a silent glide,
Scanning the woods where he resides.
Wings of gossamer, weightless and calm,
He swoops on his prey, without causing alarm.

He rises again, after a successful strike,
His favourite feast of rodent delight.
He flies to a tree and calls his mate,
Who echoes his song and awaits her sate.
The duo feed and enjoy their spoils,
Once engorged, they continue their toils.
Eerie birds, wise they are named,
Secretive with stealth, yet wild and untamed

Winter Morning

The sunshine glows in an azure sky,
Lighting sparkles as the minutes pass by.
Bright and crisp, clear and pure,
A beautiful vision with great allure.
Still and silent, this moment in time,
This breath-taking vista on the skyline.
Raising our spirits on this glorious day,
It's a precious moment and time to delay.
This morning gives a chance to unwind.
From cares and fears which fill our mind,
Basking in beams which warm the skin
Uplifting our mood and spirits within.

A Crystal Show

Bleak Winter covers the land with snow,
With hoar frosts and icicles in a crystal show.
The watery sun rays on lifeless stems
Reflect the beams on the shining gems.

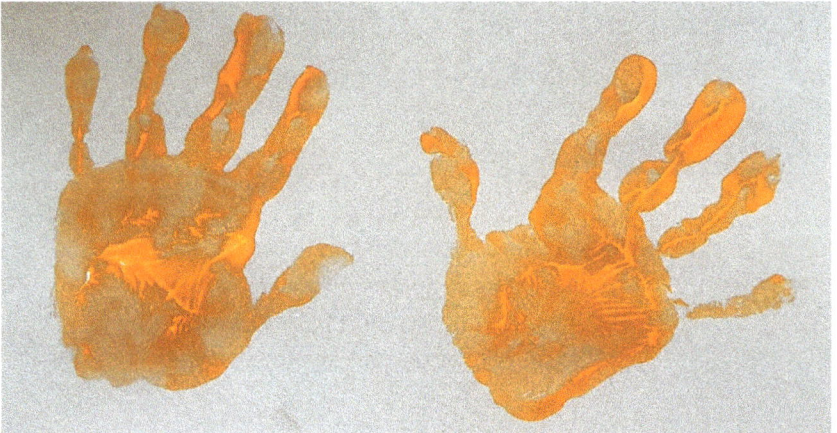

Erika's handprints aged 3 years

A Perfect Childhood

Open spaces natural and wild
great adventures for every child
wonderful woods with trees to climb
dandelion clocks to tell the time
streams to dam and fish to catch
nests to find and eggs to hatch
ponds to dip and frogs to find
great enjoyment to fill our mind
mud to ooze and make a pie
a spider to watch as he eats a fly
wiggling worms to scare your Mum
the great outdoors is such good fun
daisy chains and flowers to press
a princess robe from Gran's old dress
imagined pirates and robbers galore
sailing a ship to a distant shore
these are the days we grow and thrive
a perfect childhood,
WE FEEL SO ALIVE!
(for Erika)

Haiku Poems

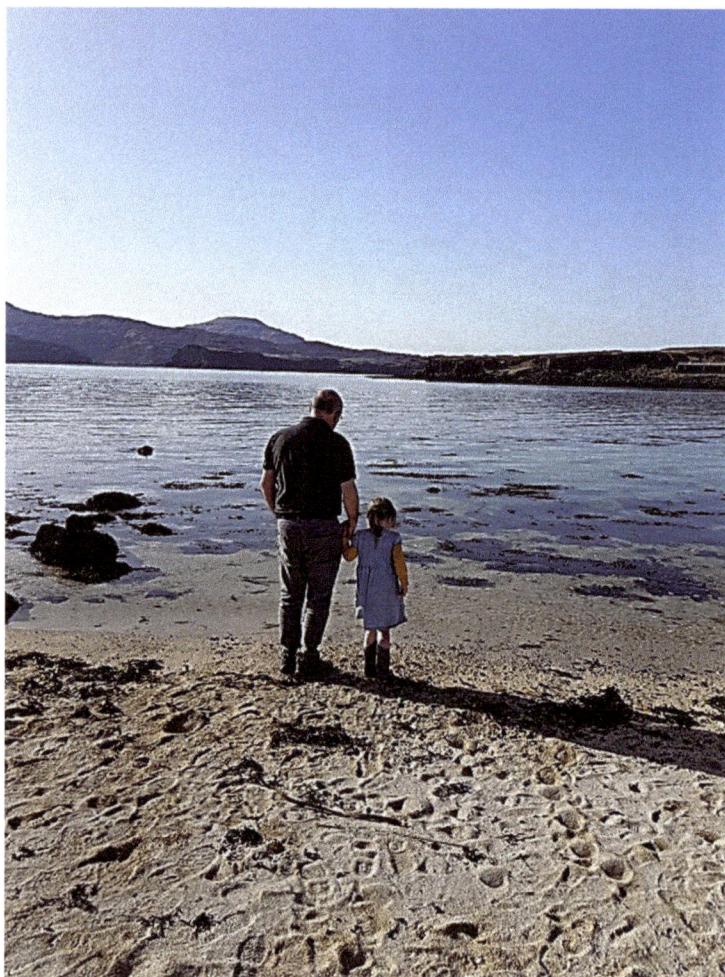

Mankind

We are one species,
amongst a million more,
we should care for all.

Bees

Man needs bees to live
to pollinate plants and trees,
save them or we fade.

Timeless Shores
Sue Wood

The Ocean

Ocean tides begin
with the drawing from the moon
ending on our shores.

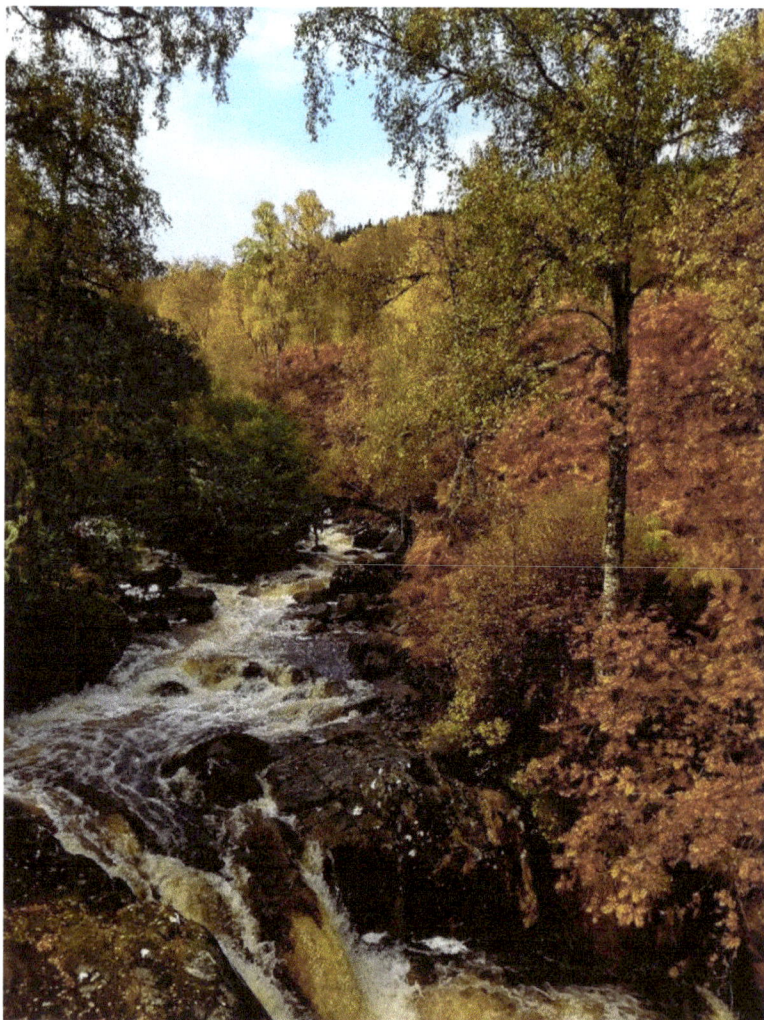

The River

The river sprays bronze
over rocks, rises and dips
for eternity.

Frost

Iced diamonds glitter,
as sunbeams shine through the gems,
a jewelled vision.

White Flower

This pure white beauty
Shines brightly in the dark glade
Light within the gloom.

Butterflies

Adorning the sky,
like tiny fires burning,
lighting up our world.

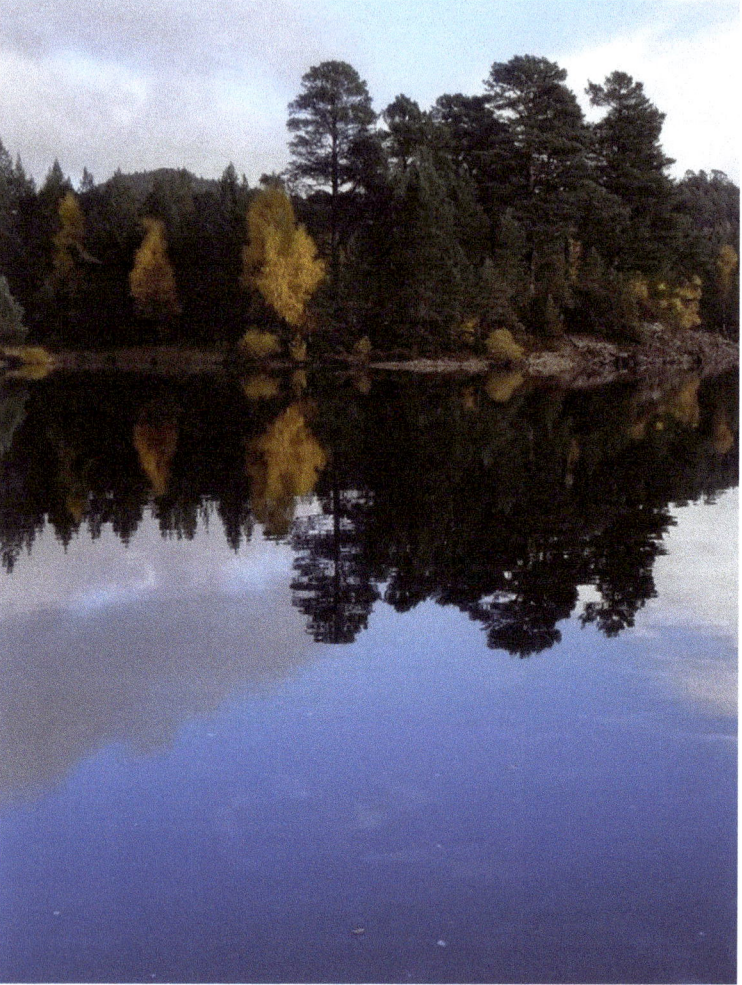

The Loch

Vast expanse which glows
Shimmering waves move with tides
Translucent mirror

Silver Birch

Snowy branches glow
Against vibrant golden leaves
Dancing in the breeze

Misty Morning

Mist rolls from the sea
natures pure veil of splendor
which shimmers with grace

Foxgloves

Spires of pink and cream
Speckled throats for bees to rest
Goblets of nectar

The Dipper

Frothy rapids flow
As he dips and dives beneath
Searching for his prey

Old Scots Pine

High up in the glen
Arching branches spreading wide
Standing strong with pride.

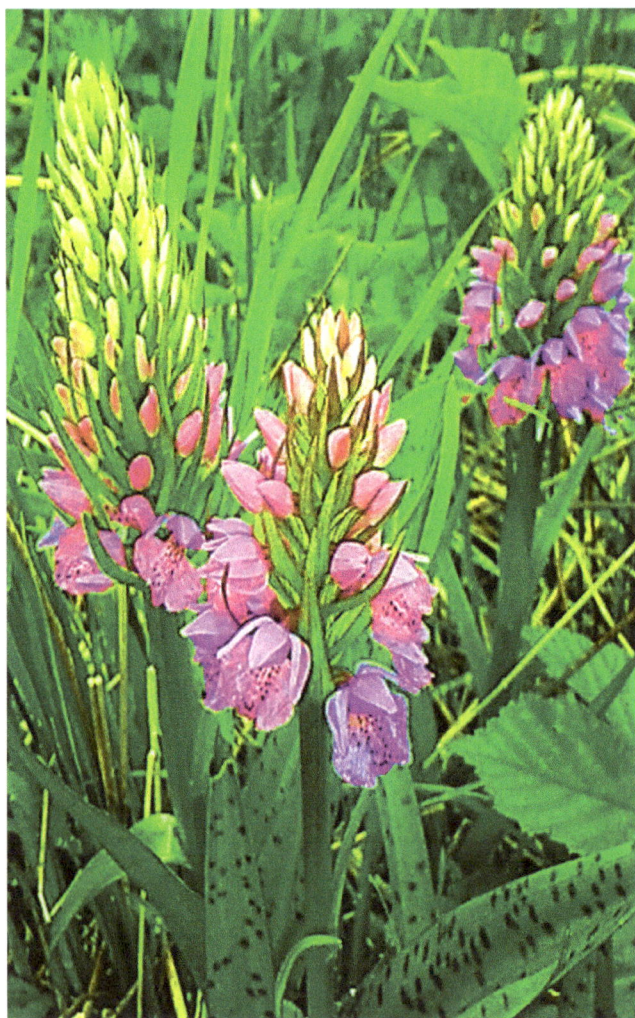

Orchids

The purple blooms glow
Ornate majestic sceptres
Fill the air with scent

Wily Fox

With bright pensive eyes
Eagle-eyed and vigilant
An opportunist

Snowflakes

Swirling and twisting
Gently floating from the sky
Covers the cold land

Pipistrelle Bat

Hunting in the air
He swoops and dives after prey
An Evening gymnast

Fly Agaric

Vibrant ruby orbs
Lighting the glade beneath the trees
Autumn's special show

Cumulonimbus

Thunder clouds gather
A threatening dark canopy
Rumbling overhead

"Enjoy the Natural World"

Sue

About the Author

I grew up in England and was fortunate enough to live in an area surrounded by farmland and open spaces. My childhood was packed full of outdoor play; building camps, making mud pies, creating perfume from rose petals and having lots of freedom. My environment was full of the natural world with an abundance of birds, beetles and wild flowers. My Father took me and my siblings blackberry picking and pond dipping on a regular basis. These were very happy times, which gave me the love of nature; a happy place to enjoy and in which to feel at home. In so many ways this was an idyllic childhood, which is now quite scarce. It was a magical time and enhanced my fascination with the natural world, which provided an environment to recharge my batteries during some difficult times. Nature is perfect for improving mental health and putting things into perspective.

Throughout my career I have always worked with pre-school children in education settings and with students in further education. I completed Child and Youth studies to gain my degree and followed this with a diploma in teaching in further education. I was an early years lecturer for the University of Highlands and Islands (UHI) in Portree.

My main focus throughout my career has been to promote the importance of the natural world for children's happiness, health and wellbeing. Once children have been fully engaged into the natural world, they will take this forward into adulthood. This is a wonderful gift, which is a natural tonic and can help protect physical and mental health for life.

When I spend time in the natural World I feel so relaxed and calm. This is my happy place and I cannot stress how wonderful walking in the countryside improves my mental health and happiness. In nature you can be in the moment and forget about everything because, you are surrounded by beauty and fascinating species of plants and wildlife.

I have lived on the Isle of Skye for 25 years and I am now fortunate to own a wildflower meadow adjacent to the banks of the river Roskhill. I named this meadow Òran Uisge (Song of Water) because, while sitting amongst the wild flowers, the river gently flows along, towards the sea, providing a tranquil sound. Òran Uisge is an inspirational place to watch the bees and butterflies foraging for food, enjoying fragrance from the wildflowers filling the air and listening to the abundance of songbirds. This wonderful setting inspired me to write my second poetry book *Òran Uisge-Wildflower Meadow*.

This collection includes; *Midsummer Night, Summer Rain, The Call from the Wild* and *The Plumed Spectre*.

"Freefall into nature
and embrace it.
A true companion for life".
Sue

Other Books by Sue Wood

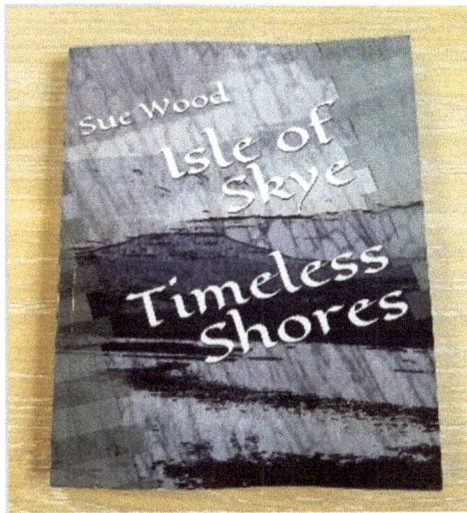

Timeless Shores is a poetic journey describing the natural wonders and culture on the Isle of Skye. Each poem is enhanced by a colourful image of a painting, drawing or photograph. The poems are written in an evocative way to allow the reader to enjoy Skye's natural wonders and colourful characters through verse.

ISBN 9798616110480

List of Illustrations

www.ingramcontent.com/pod-product-compliance
Lightning Source LLC
LaVergne TN
LVHW010309070426
835511LV00021B/3453